What Animals Eat

PETER SLOAN &
SHERYL SLOAN

The bear is a
meat eater.
It hunts small animals.

The wolf is a
meat eater.
It hunts other animals.

The crocodile is a
meat eater.
It hunts small and large
animals.

The koala is a
plant eater.
It eats gum leaves.

The goat is a
plant eater.
It eats hay and leaves.

The squirrel is a
plant eater.
It eats nuts and berries.

The rabbit is a
plant eater.
It eats grass and leaves.